THE ULTIMATE WEDDING PLANNER

YOUR GUIDE TO CREATING THE PERFECT DAY, "INCLUDING A CHAPTER ON HOW TO PICK A WEDDING THEME"

BY

YVETTE HARRIS

TABLE OF CONTENTS

INTRODUCTION

Congratulations on your engagement! As you embark on this journey toward your wedding day, you're about to embark on one of the most exciting and memorable experiences of your life. Planning a wedding can be both exhilarating and overwhelming, with countless details to consider and decisions to make. That's where "The Ultimate Wedding Planner: Your Guide to Creating the Perfect Day" comes in.

In this comprehensive guide, we're here to walk you through every step of the wedding planning process, offering expert advice, practical tips, and creative inspiration to help you craft the wedding of your dreams. From setting your budget and creating your guest list to choosing the perfect venue and selecting your wedding vendors, each chapter is designed to equip you with the knowledge and tools you need to plan with confidence.

One of the most exciting aspects of planning your wedding is selecting a theme that reflects your unique style and personality as a couple. Your chosen theme will set the tone for every aspect of your celebration, from the invitations and décor to the attire and entertainment. In the following chapters, we'll delve into the art of picking a wedding theme, offering guidance on how to find inspiration, narrow down your options, and bring your vision to life.

Whether you envision a romantic garden affair, a glamorous black-tie soirée, or a whimsical rustic celebration, "The Ultimate Wedding Planner" is here to help you navigate the planning process with ease and confidence. So sit back, relax, and lct's begin this exciting journey toward creating the perfect day for you and your loved ones

CHAPTER 1

INTRODUCTION

OVERVIEW OF THE SIGNIFICANCE OF WEDDINGS

Weddings are timeless celebrations that mark the union of two individuals in love, symbolizing the beginning of a lifelong journey together. More than just a ceremony, weddings hold profound cultural, social, and emotional significance across societies worldwide. At their core, weddings are a testament to the power of love, commitment, and community.

First and foremost, weddings serve as a public declaration of love and commitment between two people. They provide a formal opportunity for couples to express their devotion to each other in front of family, friends, and loved ones, reinforcing the bond they share and affirming their commitment to a shared future.

Weddings are deeply ingrained in cultural and religious traditions, each with its own rituals and symbolism. These traditions not only add richness and depth to the ceremony but also serve to honor heritage, ancestors, and community values. From exchanging vows to performing rituals and ceremonies, weddings reflect the customs and beliefs that have been passed down through generations, connecting the past with the present and the future.

Beyond the couple themselves, weddings are also significant social events that bring people together in celebration. They provide an opportunity for families and friends to come together, strengthen bonds, and create lasting memories. Whether it's the joyous laughter, heartfelt speeches, or lively dances, weddings foster a sense of unity and belonging that transcends individual differences and celebrates the collective joy of love and partnership.

Weddings represent the culmination of dreams, hopes, and aspirations, encapsulating the essence of love, commitment, and community. As we embark on this journey to explore the significance of weddings, let us delve deeper into the rituals, traditions, and emotions that make these celebrations truly unforgettable.

IMPORTANCE OF A WELL-PLANNED WEDDING

A well-planned wedding is not merely an event; it is a culmination of dreams, emotions, and meticulous organization. In the kaleidoscope of life's celebrations, few moments rival the significance of a wedding day. Beyond the romantic allure and ceremonial grandeur lies a fundamental truth: the importance of thoughtful planning.

A wedding represents the union of two individuals, their families, and their shared vision for the future. It is a day imbued with profound symbolism and cultural significance, where traditions intertwine with personal narratives to create a unique tapestry of love and commitment. However, orchestrating such a multifaceted occasion requires foresight, attention to detail, and a strategic approach.

A well-planned wedding sets the stage for a seamless and memorable experience for all involved. From the intricacies of guest list management to the selection of the perfect venue, every decision contributes to the overall ambiance and success of the celebration. Moreover, effective planning ensures that logistical challenges are minimized, allowing the focus to remain squarely on the joyous union of the couple.

Beyond the logistical considerations, a well-planned wedding fosters a sense of cohesion and unity among all participants. It provides a framework for collaboration and shared responsibility, empowering couples to navigate the complexities of the planning process with confidence and grace. Ultimately, the journey towards a well-planned wedding is as enriching as the destination itself, offering couples an opportunity for growth, reflection, and deepened connection.

We will explore the myriad facets of wedding planning, offering insights, tips, and inspiration to guide you on your journey towards creating the perfect day. For in the tapestry of love, every stitch of planning is a thread that binds hearts together, weaving a story that will be cherished for a lifetime.

BRIEF OUTLINE OF THE BOOK'S CONTENTS

Embark on a journey towards your dream wedding with "The Ultimate Wedding Planner: Your Guide to Creating the Perfect Day." This comprehensive book is designed to be your trusted companion throughout the exhilarating and sometimes overwhelming process of planning your special day.

1. **Setting the stage:** Explore the significance of weddings and the importance of meticulous planning. Gain insight into how this guide will equip you with the tools and knowledge needed to orchestrate a memorable celebration.

2. **Understanding Your Vision:** Learn how to articulate your wedding vision and translate it into tangible plans. Discover the significance of personalization and tailoring your wedding to reflect your unique love story.

3. **Navigating Logistics:** Delve into the practical aspects of wedding planning, from budgeting and guest list management to selecting venues and vendors. Gain valuable tips for making informed decisions and maximizing your resources.

4. **Crafting Meaningful Moments:** Explore the art of infusing personal touches and meaningful rituals into your wedding day. Discover how to create an atmosphere that resonates with your personality and values.

5. **Embracing the Journey:** Prepare yourself for the emotional rollercoaster of wedding planning. Learn strategies for managing stress, navigating conflicts, and staying focused on what truly matters.

CHAPTER 2

SETTING YOUR BUDGET

UNDERSTANDING THE FINANCIAL ASPECTS OF WEDDING PLANNING

Understanding the financial aspects of wedding planning, particularly setting a budget, is crucial for couples embarking on their journey toward matrimony. Setting a budget involves more than just determining a total spending limit; it requires careful consideration of various expenses and priorities. Firstly, couples should assess their financial situation realistically, taking into account their income, savings, and any contributions from family members. Next, they must decide on the overall amount they are willing to allocate to their wedding, considering factors such as their desired guest count, venue preferences, and level of extravagance.

Once the total budget is established, it's essential to break it down into categories to allocate funds accordingly. These categories may include venue and catering, attire, photography and videography, entertainment, decorations, and miscellaneous expenses. Prioritizing these categories based on personal preferences helps ensure that essential elements receive adequate funding while allowing for flexibility in less critical areas.

Setting up a contingency fund is wise to accommodate unexpected costs that may arise during the planning process. It's essential to be mindful of not only the initial expenses but also ongoing payments, such as vendor deposits and final payments.

Regularly revisiting and adjusting the budget throughout the planning process is crucial to staying on track and avoiding overspending. Utilizing budgeting tools, spreadsheets, or wedding planning apps can aid in this process, providing visual representations of expenses and helping to monitor expenditures effectively.

CREATING A REALISTIC BUDGET

Setting a realistic budget is the cornerstone of successful wedding planning, ensuring that your vision for the perfect day aligns with your financial resources. The process begins with a thorough examination of your financial situation, including your savings, income, and any contributions from family members. Establishing a clear budget early on allows you to make informed decisions and prioritize your spending accordingly.

To set a budget that works for you, start by listing all potential expenses associated with your wedding, including venue rental, catering, attire, entertainment, and decorations. Research typical costs for each item in your area to develop a realistic estimate. It's essential to be comprehensive and account for any hidden fees or unexpected expenses that may arise.

Once you have a rough budget in mind, determine your top priorities and allocate funds accordingly. Decide which aspects of your wedding are non-negotiable and where you're willing to compromise. Remember to set aside a contingency fund to cover any unforeseen costs that may arise during the planning process.

Throughout the planning process, track your spending carefully to ensure that you stay within your budgetary limits. Consider using budgeting tools or spreadsheets to monitor expenses and make adjustments as needed. Be prepared to make trade-offs or adjustments to your plans if necessary to avoid overspending.

Communication is key when it comes to budgeting for your wedding. Be open and honest with your partner and any family members contributing financially, discussing priorities, concerns, and any financial constraints. By setting a realistic budget and sticking to it, you can ensure that your wedding day is both memorable and financially manageable.

TIPS FOR STICKING TO YOUR BUDGET THROUGHOUT THE PLANNING PROCESS

Sticking to your budget throughout the wedding planning process is crucial for maintaining financial stability and reducing stress. Here are some tips to help you set a realistic budget and stay on track:

Define Your Priorities: Determine what aspects of your wedding are most important to you and allocate a larger portion of your budget to those elements. Whether it's the venue, photography, or entertainment, knowing your priorities will guide your spending decisions.

Research Costs: Take the time to research the average cost of wedding essentials in your area. Understanding typical expenses for venues, catering, attire, and other services will help you set a budget that aligns with your financial resources.

Create a Detailed Budget Spreadsheet: Use a spreadsheet or budgeting tool to create a comprehensive list of all wedding expenses, including both major and minor items. Assign each expense a specific amount, and regularly update your spreadsheet to track your spending and ensure you stay within your budget limits.

Include contingency funds: factor in a buffer for unexpected expenses or last-minute changes. Having a contingency fund of around 10–15% of your total budget will provide financial flexibility and help you avoid overspending.

Negotiate and prioritize: Don't be afraid to negotiate with vendors to secure the best possible prices. Consider alternatives or compromises for elements that exceed your budget, and prioritize your spending on items that are most meaningful to you and your partner.

Stick to Your Limits: Resist the temptation to overspend on unnecessary extras or impulse purchases. Stay disciplined and refer back to your budget spreadsheet regularly to remind yourself of your financial goals and constraints.

CHAPTER 3

CREATING YOUR GUEST LIST

STRATEGIES FOR DETERMINING WHO TO INVITE

Creating a guest list is a crucial aspect of wedding planning, ensuring that the celebration is shared with the right people. To effectively determine who to invite, several strategic approaches can be employed.

Consider immediate family and close friends. These are the individuals who have played significant roles in your life and whose presence is essential on your special day. Start by listing these individuals to establish a core group of guests.

Think about extended family members and acquaintances. While it's natural to want to include everyone, practical considerations such as venue capacity and budget constraints may necessitate prioritization. Focus on those with whom you have regular contact or strong relationships.

Consider the purpose of your wedding. Are you envisioning an intimate gathering or a grand celebration? Your wedding's scale and style will influence the size of your guest list. For a more intimate affair, prioritize close connections, while larger-scale weddings may accommodate a broader range of guests.

Be mindful of potential conflicts or dynamics among guests. While it's impossible to please everyone, consider the potential impact of inviting certain individuals on the overall atmosphere of the event. Strive for a harmonious mix of guests who will contribute positively to the celebration.

Finally, maintain flexibility throughout the process. It's natural for guest lists to evolve as planning progresses. Regularly revisit and refine your list, keeping in mind your priorities and vision for the day.

MANAGING GUEST LIST CONFLICTS

Managing guest list conflicts is a crucial aspect of wedding planning, ensuring a harmonious and enjoyable celebration for all involved. When creating your guest list, it's essential to approach the process with sensitivity and diplomacy.

Establish clear criteria for who will be invited, considering factors such as familial obligations, budget constraints, and venue capacity. Communicate openly with your partner and family to align expectations and avoid misunderstandings later on.

Anticipate potential conflicts that may arise, such as disagreements over inviting distant relatives, ex-partners, or friends who may not get along. Address these issues proactively by setting boundaries and making compromises where necessary.

In cases where space or budget constraints prevent inviting everyone, prioritize individuals who play significant roles in your lives and have been supportive of your relationship. Consider hosting separate events or celebrations to include additional guests without compromising the intimacy of your wedding day.

When faced with objections or requests for additional invitations, handle them tactfully and assertively. Explain your reasoning behind the guest list decisions and reassure concerned parties of your appreciation for their understanding.

Throughout the process, maintain open lines of communication with all stakeholders and be prepared to listen to their perspectives. Remember that while it's impossible to please everyone, prioritizing your vision for the day and the comfort of you and your partner is paramount. By approaching guest list management with empathy, diplomacy, and clear communication, you can navigate conflicts gracefully and create a memorable wedding experience for all involved.

TOOLS AND TEMPLATES FOR ORGANIZING YOUR GUEST LIST

Organizing your guest list is a critical aspect of wedding planning, ensuring that your special day is shared with those who matter most to you. To facilitate this process, several tools and templates can streamline the creation and management of your guest list.

Digital spreadsheet software like Microsoft Excel or Google Sheets provides a versatile platform for organizing guest information. With customizable columns for names, addresses, RSVP status, dietary preferences, and more, these tools allow for efficient sorting and filtering as you compile your list.

Specialized wedding planning websites and apps offer guest list management features. These platforms often include pre-designed templates tailored for weddings, simplifying the task of inputting guest details and tracking RSVPs. Some apps even integrate with online invitation services, making it easy to send out invites and receive responses electronically.

Printable guest list templates are available for those who prefer a tangible format. These templates typically include sections for essential details like guest names, contact information, and meal preferences, providing a convenient way to organize information offline.

As you create your guest list, consider categorizing guests into groups, such as family, friends, coworkers, and acquaintances. This segmentation can help you allocate seating arrangements, manage event logistics, and prioritize invitations within your budget.

CHAPTER **4**

CHOOSING THE PERFECT VENUE

FACTORS TO CONSIDER WHEN SELECTING A VENUE

Selecting the perfect venue for your wedding is a crucial decision that can significantly impact the overall atmosphere and experience of your special day. Several key factors should be considered to ensure that you choose a venue that aligns with your vision and meets your practical needs.

Consider the size and capacity of the venue. Ensure that it can comfortably accommodate your anticipated number of guests while also allowing for any additional space needed for activities such as dancing or dining.

Location plays a vital role in the overall convenience and accessibility of your venue. Consider factors such as proximity to transportation hubs, accommodations for out-of-town guests, and the overall ambiance of the surrounding area.

Evaluate the amenities and facilities offered by the venue. Look for features such as on-site catering, audiovisual equipment, bridal suites, and outdoor spaces for ceremonies or receptions. These amenities can enhance the convenience and enjoyment of your wedding day for both you and your guests.

Consider the aesthetic appeal and ambiance of the venue. Choose a setting that reflects your personal style and complements the overall theme or mood of your wedding. Whether you prefer a rustic barn, a chic urban loft, or a picturesque garden, the ambiance of the venue will set the tone for your entire celebration.

And don't forget to consider the budgetary implications of your venue choice. Ensure that the cost of the venue aligns with your overall budget and that there are no hidden fees or unexpected expenses.

DIFFERENT TYPES OF VENUES AND THEIR PROS AND CONS

When it comes to choosing the perfect venue for your wedding, there are various types to consider, each with its own set of pros and cons. Understanding these options can help you make an informed decision that aligns with your vision and budget.

HOTELS AND RESORTS:

Pros: Convenient for out-of-town guests, often offer all-inclusive packages including catering and accommodations, experienced staff for seamless coordination.

Cons: May lack uniqueness and personalization, limited flexibility in décor and vendor choices, potentially higher cost.

HISTORIC VENUES:

Pros: Charm and character, stunning architecture and picturesque surroundings, ideal for couples seeking a romantic, vintage atmosphere.

Cons: Limited availability due to popularity, may have restrictions on customization, additional costs for amenities and services.

OUTDOOR VENUES:

Pros: Natural beauty and scenic views, ample space for large guest lists, flexibility in design and layout, perfect for couples who love nature.

Cons: Weather dependency, additional costs for rentals like tents and restrooms, may require permits and insurance.

BANQUET HALLS

Pros: Spacious and versatile, often come with catering services and amenities, customizable to match your theme and décor.

Cons: Lack of uniqueness, may feel impersonal, limited outdoor space for ceremonies or photography.

DESTINATION VENUES:

Pros: Memorable experience for couples and guests, beautiful settings for ceremonies and receptions, potential for extended celebrations.

Cons: Travel logistics for guests, higher costs for travel and accommodations, limited options for local vendors.

Choosing the perfect venue involves weighing these pros and cons against your priorities, budget, and overall wedding vision. Conducting thorough research, visiting potential venues, and asking pertinent questions will help you find the ideal setting to bring your dream wedding to life.

TIPS FOR NEGOTIATING CONTRACTS AND SECURING YOUR DATE

When negotiating contracts and securing your wedding date, choosing the perfect venue requires attention to detail and effective communication. ***Here are some essential tips to consider:***

Research and Compare: Begin by researching different venues that match your vision and budget. Compare their offerings, including amenities, capacity, and pricing packages.

Flexibility: Be flexible with your wedding date, especially if you have a preferred venue in mind. Off-peak seasons or weekdays may offer more availability and potentially lower costs.

Ask Questions: During venue tours or consultations, ask detailed questions about what is included in the venue rental fee. Inquire about any restrictions, such as catering options, décor guidelines, or noise ordinances.

Review Contracts Thoroughly: Carefully review all contracts and agreements before signing. Pay close attention to cancellation policies, payment schedules, and any additional fees or charges.

Negotiate Terms: Don't hesitate to negotiate terms that are favorable to you, such as discounts, complimentary upgrades, or flexible payment plans. Highlight any specific requests or requirements you have for your wedding day.

Get Everything in Writing: Ensure that all agreements, changes, and additions are documented in writing. This includes any verbal agreements made during negotiations.

Consider Venue Reputation: Research the venue's reputation by reading reviews and testimonials from past clients. Pay attention to feedback regarding responsiveness, reliability, and overall satisfaction.

Visit Multiple Times: Schedule multiple visits to your chosen venue to familiarize yourself with the space and envision your wedding day. Take note of lighting, layout, and any potential logistical challenges.

By following these tips and maintaining open communication with venue representatives, you can negotiate contracts effectively and secure the perfect venue for your special day.

CHAPTER **5**

SELECTING YOUR WEDDING THEME

EXPLORING DIFFERENT WEDDING THEMES AND STYLES

Selecting a wedding theme is a pivotal step in the wedding planning process, as it sets the tone and style for the entire celebration. There is a plethora of wedding themes and styles to choose from, each offering a unique atmosphere and ambiance.

Couples should consider their personal interests, passions, and personalities. Whether it's a rustic barn wedding, a glamorous black-tie affair, or a whimsical garden party, the chosen theme should resonate with the couple and reflect their individuality. Additionally, cultural background, shared hobbies, and favorite memories can serve as inspiration for the wedding theme.

The venue plays a crucial role in determining the appropriate theme. A beachfront resort may inspire a tropical or nautical theme, while a historic mansion lends itself to a vintage or classic theme. Couples should consider how the chosen theme complements the venue's existing aesthetics and ambiance.

Couples should think about the season and time of year when selecting a wedding theme. A winter wonderland theme is perfect for a December wedding, while a vibrant and colorful theme suits a summer celebration.

Practical considerations such as budget, availability of décor elements, and feasibility of execution should not be overlooked. DIY elements, rental options,

18

and creative alternatives can help bring the chosen theme to life within budget constraints.

HOW TO CHOOSE A THEME THAT REFLECTS YOUR PERSONALITY AND INTERESTS

Selecting a wedding theme that resonates with your personality and interests is a crucial step in creating a memorable and cohesive wedding experience. To choose the perfect theme, start by reflecting on your personal style, interests, and shared experiences as a couple. Consider elements such as your favorite colors, hobbies, cultural backgrounds, and meaningful locations that hold significance to both of you.

Brainstorm ideas that align with these aspects of your lives. Think about themes that evoke the feelings and atmosphere you envision for your special day. Whether it's rustic charm, vintage elegance, modern sophistication, or a whimsical fairytale, your theme should reflect your unique tastes and preferences.

Draw inspiration from your love story and shared experiences. Consider incorporating elements that symbolize important milestones, such as where you met, your favorite travel destinations, or shared hobbies. Infusing personal touches into your theme will make your wedding feel truly authentic and meaningful.

Think about practical considerations such as the season, location, and venue of your wedding. Your theme should complement the overall aesthetic of your chosen venue and blend seamlessly with the surroundings.

Don't be afraid to get creative and think outside the box. Your wedding theme should be a reflection of your individuality as a couple, so don't feel limited by traditional notions of what a wedding should be. Trust your instincts, follow your hearts, and choose a theme that speaks to you both, ensuring that your wedding day is a true reflection of your love story.

INCORPORATING CULTURAL OR FAMILY TRADITIONS INTO YOUR THEME

Incorporating cultural or family traditions into your wedding theme adds depth, meaning, and personalization to your special day. When selecting your wedding theme, consider the rich tapestry of traditions that have shaped your heritage or family history. ***Here's a structured approach to integrating cultural or familial elements into your wedding theme:***

Research and Reflection: Begin by researching the cultural or familial traditions that resonate with you and your partner. Reflect on the customs, rituals, and symbols that hold significance within your heritage or family background.

Identify Key Traditions: Identify key traditions that you wish to incorporate into your wedding theme. These could include ceremonies, attire, music, cuisine, or decor elements that reflect your cultural or familial heritage.

Adaptation and Modernization: Adapt traditional elements to suit your personal style and preferences. Modernize customs or rituals to align with the overall aesthetic and atmosphere of your wedding.

Integration with Theme: Integrate cultural or familial traditions seamlessly into your chosen wedding theme. Ensure that these elements complement the overall look and feel of your celebration while adding depth and authenticity.

Consultation and Collaboration: Consult with family members or cultural experts to ensure respectful and accurate representation of traditions. Collaborate with wedding vendors, such as planners, decorators, and caterers, to incorporate cultural or familial elements into every aspect of your wedding day.

Education and Inclusion: Educate your guests about the significance of the cultural or familial traditions woven into your wedding theme. Create opportunities for participation and inclusion, allowing guests to experience and appreciate the richness of your heritage or family background.

CHAPTER **6**

FINDING THE RIGHT VENDORS

IDENTIFYING AND HIRING THE BEST VENDORS FOR YOUR WEDDING

Finding the right vendors for your wedding is a crucial step in ensuring that your special day goes smoothly and meets your expectations. The process involves thorough research, careful consideration of your needs and preferences, and effective communication. *Here's a structured guide to help you identify and hire the best vendors for your wedding*:

Define Your Needs: Start by identifying the specific services you require for your wedding, such as photography, catering, florals, music, and transportation. Determine your budget for each service to guide your search.

Research: Utilize online resources, such as wedding vendor directories, review websites, and social media platforms, to compile a list of potential vendors in your area. Seek recommendations from friends, family, and wedding professionals.

Read Reviews: Take the time to read reviews and testimonials from previous clients to gauge the quality of service provided by each vendor. Look for consistency in positive feedback and pay attention to any recurring issues or concerns mentioned.

Review Portfolios: Explore the portfolios or galleries of vendors to assess their style, creativity, and attention to detail. Look for examples of their work that resonate with your vision for your wedding.

Schedule Consultations: Reach out to your shortlisted vendors to schedule consultations or meetings. Use this opportunity to discuss your needs, ask questions, and assess their professionalism, responsiveness, and compatibility with your personality and vision.

Ask for References: Request references from past clients to gain insight into their overall experience with the vendor. Contact these references to inquire about their satisfaction with the vendor's services and professionalism.

Review Contracts: Carefully review contracts and agreements provided by vendors to ensure clarity regarding services, pricing, payment schedules, cancellation policies, and any additional terms or conditions.

By following these steps and taking a diligent approach to finding the right vendors, you can assemble a reliable team of professionals who will contribute to making your wedding day truly memorable.

QUESTIONS TO ASK POTENTIAL VENDORS

When searching for the perfect vendors to bring your wedding vision to life, asking the right questions is crucial. *Here's a structured guide to help you find the right vendors for your big day:*

Experience and Expertise: Inquire about the vendor's experience in the wedding industry and their expertise in handling events similar to yours. Ask for references or examples of past work to gauge their proficiency.

Availability and Flexibility: Confirm the vendor's availability on your wedding date and discuss their flexibility in accommodating any specific requests or changes you may have.

Services Offered: Clarify the range of services offered by the vendor and what is included in their packages. Understand any additional costs or customization options available.

Contract and Policies: Review the vendor's contract thoroughly, paying attention to cancellation policies, payment schedules, and any other terms and conditions. Seek clarification on any ambiguous clauses before signing.

Communication and Collaboration: Discuss the vendor's communication style and preferred methods of contact. Ensure that they are responsive and open to collaboration throughout the planning process.

Backup Plans: Inquire about the vendor's contingency plans in case of emergencies or unforeseen circumstances. It's essential to know how they handle last-minute changes or issues on the wedding day.

Logistics and Setup: Discuss logistical details such as setup and teardown times, space requirements, and any specific venue restrictions or regulations that may affect their services.

Reviews and Testimonials: Ask for client testimonials or reviews from previous weddings to gain insight into the vendor's professionalism, reliability, and quality of service.

Insurance and Licenses: Ensure that the vendor carries proper insurance coverage and any necessary licenses or permits required by your venue or local authorities.

Personal Connection: Finally, trust your instincts and assess whether you feel comfortable and confident working with the vendor. A strong rapport and personal connection can make the planning process much more enjoyable and successful.

TIPS FOR MANAGING VENDOR CONTRACTS AND PAYMENTS

When it comes to planning your wedding, selecting the right vendors is crucial to ensure a seamless and memorable experience. ***Here are some essential tips for finding the perfect vendors and managing contracts and payments effectively:***

Research Extensively: Take the time to research potential vendors thoroughly. Look for reviews, testimonials, and portfolios to gauge their quality of work and reliability.

Seek Recommendations: Ask friends, family, and recently married couples for recommendations. Personal referrals can provide valuable insights into the professionalism and expertise of vendors.

Meet in Person or Virtually: Schedule meetings with potential vendors to discuss your vision, preferences, and budget. Whether in person or virtually, these meetings offer an opportunity to assess compatibility and communication style.

Review Contracts Carefully: Once you've chosen your vendors, review their contracts carefully. Pay attention to important details such as services provided, pricing, payment schedule, cancellation policies, and deadlines.

Clarify Expectations: Clearly communicate your expectations and preferences with each vendor. Discuss specific details such as timelines, deliverables, setup requirements, and any customization options.

Negotiate Terms: Don't hesitate to negotiate terms that are favorable to both parties. Be open and transparent about your budget constraints and any special requests.

Secure Payment Plans: Agree on a payment schedule that works for both you and the vendor. Consider making a deposit to secure their services, with the remaining balance due at specified intervals or upon completion of services.

Keep Records: Maintain organized records of all contracts, payments, and correspondence with vendors. This will help you stay on top of deadlines and ensure accountability throughout the planning process.

CHAPTER **7**

DESIGNING YOUR WEDDING DÉCOR

TIPS FOR CREATING A COHESIVE AESTHETIC

Designing your wedding décor is an essential aspect of creating a cohesive aesthetic that reflects your personal style and vision for your special day. *Here are some valuable tips to ensure your wedding décor is both stunning and harmonious:*

Establish a Clear Vision: Begin by defining the overall look and feel you want to achieve for your wedding. Consider factors such as color scheme, theme, and any specific elements you want to incorporate to make your décor unique.

Create Mood Boards: Gather inspiration from magazines, Pinterest, or other sources and compile them into mood boards to visualize your ideas. This will help you communicate your vision to vendors and ensure everyone is on the same page.

Focus on Key Elements: Identify key focal points for your décor, such as the ceremony arch, reception tables, and entrance area. Allocate your budget and attention accordingly to make these areas stand out.

Consider the Venue: Take into account the architectural features and existing décor of your venue when planning your own. Choose elements that complement the space rather than clash with it.

Balance and Cohesion: Aim for a balanced and cohesive look by ensuring that all elements of your décor work together harmoniously. This includes coordinating colors, textures, and styles throughout the venue.

Personalize with Meaningful Details: Incorporate personal touches that reflect your relationship and story as a couple. This could be through family heirlooms, custom signage, or DIY decorations that hold sentimental value.

Don't Overlook Lighting: Lighting plays a crucial role in setting the mood and ambiance of your wedding. Experiment with different lighting options such as candles, string lights, or uplighting to create the desired atmosphere.

DIY DECOR IDEAS AND INSPIRATION

Designing your wedding décor allows you to infuse your special day with your unique personality and style. ***Here are some DIY décor ideas and inspiration to help you create a memorable atmosphere for your celebration:***

Personalized Signage: Craft custom signs with calligraphy or hand-lettering to welcome guests, display the schedule of events, or designate seating arrangements. Incorporate meaningful quotes, song lyrics, or inside jokes to add a personal touch.

Centerpieces with a Twist: Get creative with centerpieces by using unconventional items such as vintage books, lanterns, or terrariums filled with succulents. Mix and match textures, heights, and colors to add visual interest to your tables.

Handcrafted Garlands: Create your own garlands using materials like fresh flowers, paper, or fabric. Hang them along the ceremony aisle, drape them across tables, or use them to adorn the backs of chairs for a whimsical touch.

Photo Displays: Share your love story with guests by showcasing photos of you and your partner throughout the years. Arrange them in vintage frames, hang them from a rustic ladder, or create a photo wall with strings and clothespins.

DIY Lighting: Set the mood with homemade lighting elements such as mason jar lanterns, string lights, or candlelit luminaries. Experiment with different placements and intensities to create a warm and inviting ambiance.

Nature-Inspired Accents: Incorporate elements from nature such as branches, leaves, or driftwood into your décor. Use them to embellish centerpieces, create table runners, or adorn ceremony arches for a rustic and organic feel.

Up cycled Décor: Give new life to old items by repurposing them into wedding decorations. Transform vintage suitcases into card holders, turn wine bottles into candleholders, or use old windows as seating charts.

WORKING WITH A PROFESSIONAL DECORATOR OR STYLIST

Engaging a professional decorator or stylist for your wedding décor can transform your venue into a breathtaking setting that perfectly encapsulates your vision for the day. These experts bring creativity, experience, and attention to detail, ensuring that every element harmonizes seamlessly to create a stunning ambiance.

Initial Consultation: The process typically begins with an initial consultation, where you discuss your ideas, preferences, and budget with the decorator or stylist. This is an opportunity to convey your vision and style, while also benefitting from their expertise and suggestions.

Concept Development: Based on your preferences and theme, the decorator will develop a comprehensive design concept for your wedding décor. This may include color schemes, floral arrangements, lighting designs, and other decorative elements tailored to your venue and personal taste.

Customization and Personalization: A professional decorator will work closely with you to customize and personalize every aspect of your wedding décor. Whether it's incorporating sentimental items, family heirlooms, or unique cultural elements, they ensure that your wedding reflects your personality and story.

Execution and Installation: On the day of your wedding, the decorator or stylist takes charge of executing the design plan. From setting up elaborate floral displays to arranging table settings and draping fabrics, they handle every detail with precision and care.

Coordination with Other Vendors: Professional decorators often collaborate closely with other vendors, such as florists, rental companies, and venue staff, to ensure smooth coordination and execution of the design plan.

CHAPTER 8

PLANNING YOUR CEREMONY

STRUCTURING YOUR CEREMONY

Planning your wedding ceremony is a pivotal aspect of creating a memorable and meaningful celebration of love. Structuring your ceremony requires thoughtful consideration of various elements to ensure that it reflects your values, beliefs, and relationship dynamics. ***Here's a structured approach to planning your ceremony:***

Define Your Vision: Begin by envisioning the type of ceremony you desire. Consider whether you prefer a traditional religious ceremony, a secular celebration, or a blend of both. Discuss your vision with your partner to ensure alignment and mutual understanding.

Select Officiant: Choose an officiant who resonates with your beliefs and personalities. Whether it's a religious leader, a friend ordained for the occasion, or a professional officiant, ensure they understand your vision for the ceremony and are willing to personalize it accordingly.

Craft the Ceremony Outline: Collaborate with your officiant to outline the structure of the ceremony. Decide on key elements such as opening words, vows, ring exchange, readings, and any rituals or traditions you wish to incorporate. Ensure the flow of the ceremony reflects your preferences and creates a meaningful experience for you and your guests.

Personalize Your Vows: Write or customize your vows to express your love, commitment, and promises to each other. Personalized vows add a heartfelt touch to the ceremony and make it uniquely yours.

Incorporate Special Touches: Infuse the ceremony with personal touches that reflect your relationship and shared experiences. This could include a favorite song, a meaningful reading, a cultural ritual, or the involvement of loved ones in significant roles.

Rehearse: Practice the ceremony with your officiant and any participants to ensure a smooth and seamless execution on the big day. Rehearsing allows you to iron out any logistical issues and feel more confident and relaxed when the moment arrives.

CHOOSING READINGS, MUSIC, AND RITUALS

Crafting the perfect wedding ceremony involves attention to every detail, from the venue to the décor. Central to this experience are the readings, music, and rituals that imbue the occasion with personal significance and emotional resonance.

READINGS: Selecting readings for your ceremony allows you to infuse it with words that hold special meaning for you as a couple. Whether it's a passage from a favorite book, a poem that speaks to your love, or a religious text that reflects your beliefs, readings offer an opportunity to share your values and emotions with your loved ones.

MUSIC: Music has the power to evoke emotion and set the tone for your ceremony. From the processional as you walk down the aisle to the recessional as you exit as a newlywed couple, each musical choice should reflect your style and preferences. Consider incorporating meaningful songs or hiring musicians to perform live for an added touch of elegance.

RITUALS: Rituals add depth and symbolism to your ceremony, celebrating your unique bond and shared commitment. Whether you opt for a traditional ritual like the lighting of a unity candle or create your own ceremony such as a sand blending or handfasting, these symbolic acts can enhance the sense of unity and connection between you and your partner.

INCORPORATING PERSONAL TOUCHES INTO YOUR CEREMONY

Your wedding ceremony serves as the heart of your celebration, symbolizing the union of two individuals and the beginning of a lifelong journey together. Infusing personal touches into this sacred event elevates its significance, creating a deeply meaningful experience for both you and your guests.

1. Reflecting Your Story: Start by reflecting on your journey as a couple. Consider incorporating elements that highlight significant moments, such as the location of your first date or the story of how you met. Sharing anecdotes and memories adds a personal touch that resonates with your loved ones.

2. Customizing Vows and Readings: Write your own vows or select readings that hold personal significance. Expressing your love and commitment in your own words adds authenticity and intimacy to the ceremony. Choose readings from literature, poetry, or religious texts that reflect your values and beliefs as a couple.

3. Honoring Loved Ones: Pay tribute to family members or friends who have played a significant role in your lives. Incorporate rituals such as lighting candles, exchanging flowers, or presenting symbolic gifts to honor their presence and influence.

4. Cultural Traditions: Embrace cultural traditions that hold meaning for you and your families. Incorporate rituals, music, or attire that reflect your cultural heritage, celebrating diversity and unity.

5. Creating Rituals: Develop unique rituals or ceremonies that symbolize your commitment and intentions as a couple. Planting a tree, releasing doves, or performing a hand fasting ceremony are just a few examples of rituals that can add depth and symbolism to your ceremony.

In planning your wedding ceremony, remember that it's a reflection of your love story and journey together. By incorporating personal touches, you create a ceremony that is truly one-of-a-kind, leaving a lasting impression on both you and your guests.

CHAPTER 9

ORGANIZING YOUR RECEPTION

PLANNING THE FLOW OF EVENTS

Organizing the reception is a pivotal aspect of wedding planning, as it sets the tone for the celebratory atmosphere that follows the ceremony. Planning the flow of events ensures that guests are engaged and entertained throughout the evening, creating unforgettable memories for everyone involved.

Organizing your reception is to establish a timeline that outlines the sequence of events, from the entrance of the newlyweds to the final farewell. This timeline should include key moments such as the grand entrance, speeches, dinner service, cake cutting, and dancing. By mapping out these events in advance, you can ensure a smooth transition from one activity to the next, keeping guests engaged and entertained.

Consider the logistics of the reception space, including seating arrangements, decor, and audiovisual requirements. Whether you're hosting a formal sit-down dinner or a casual cocktail reception, thoughtful planning is essential to creating a welcoming atmosphere for your guests.

When it comes to food and beverage service, collaborate closely with your caterer to design a menu that reflects your tastes and accommodates any dietary restrictions or preferences among your guests. Consider offering a variety of options to cater to different palates and ensure that there is plenty of food and drink to go around.

Don't forget to incorporate entertainment into your reception plan, whether it's a live band, DJ, or other performers. Music sets the mood for the evening and encourages guests to hit the dance floor, so choose entertainment that resonates with your personal style and preferences.

SELECTING A MENU AND BEVERAGES

Selecting the menu and beverages for your reception is a key element in orchestrating a memorable wedding experience. Begin by considering the preferences and dietary restrictions of your guests, aiming to provide a diverse array of options that cater to various tastes and dietary needs. Collaborating closely with your chosen caterer or venue, craft a menu that reflects your personal style and complements the overall theme of your wedding.

Start with hors d'oeuvres and appetizers to greet guests upon arrival, offering a tantalizing introduction to the culinary journey ahead. Consider incorporating a mix of hot and cold options, including both meat-based and vegetarian selections to accommodate all preferences. For the main course, present a selection of entrées that showcase a balance of flavors and textures, ensuring there's something for everyone to enjoy. Offering a choice between a few carefully curate dishes can enhance the dining experience and make guests feel valued.

When it comes to beverages, think beyond the standard options and consider incorporating signature cocktails, specialty wines, or craft beers that resonate with your taste and personality as a couple. Providing a well-stocked bar with a variety of non-alcoholic options ensures that all guests can toast to your joyous occasion in their preferred manner. Don't forget to offer alternatives for those with dietary restrictions, such as gluten-free or alcohol-free choices, to ensure everyone feels included and cared for.

ENTERTAINMENT OPTIONS FOR YOUR RECEPTION

When it comes to organizing your reception, entertainment plays a vital role in creating a memorable experience for you and your guests. Begin by considering the atmosphere you wish to cultivate, whether it's an elegant affair with live music or a lively celebration with a DJ spinning tunes. Live bands bring a dynamic energy and personal touch to the event, offering versatility in music selection and interaction with guests. Alternatively, a skilled DJ can curate playlists tailored to your preferences and keep the dance floor alive throughout the night. Interactive entertainment options such as photo booths, caricature artists, or even magicians can add whimsy and engagement to the festivities, providing guests with unforgettable moments to cherish. Additionally, consider incorporating cultural or thematic elements into the entertainment lineup to reflect your unique style and heritage. Whatever entertainment you choose, ensure proper coordination with your venue and vendors to seamlessly integrate these elements into the reception timeline. By thoughtfully selecting entertainment options that resonate with you and your partner, you can create an atmosphere of joy and celebration that will be fondly remembered by all in attendance.

CHAPTER 10

MANAGING DAY-OF LOGISTICS

CREATING A DETAILED TIMELINE FOR THE WEDDING DAY

A meticulously crafted timeline is the cornerstone of a seamlessly orchestrated wedding day. It serves as a roadmap, directing each element of the celebration and minimizing the risk of hiccups. Begin by collaborating with your wedding planner, if you have one, or assembling a team of trusted individuals to assist in the creation of the timeline.

1. Start Early: Commence drafting the timeline well in advance, incorporating input from key stakeholders such as vendors, bridal party members, and family members.

2. Detail Every Aspect: From the moment the bridal party begins preparations to the final dance of the evening, include every scheduled activity in the timeline. This encompasses hair and makeup sessions, transportation arrangements, photo sessions, ceremony proceedings, and reception events.

3. Allow Buffer Time: Factor in buffer periods between activities to accommodate unforeseen delays or last-minute adjustments. This flexibility ensures that even if minor disruptions occur, the overall schedule remains on track.

4. Communicate Effectively: Distribute copies of the finalized timeline to all relevant parties, including vendors, bridal party members, and key family members. Clear communication ensures that everyone is aware of their responsibilities and the expected timeline for the day.

5. Designate a Point Person: Appoint a responsible individual, such as the wedding planner or a trusted friend or family member, to oversee the execution of the timeline on the wedding day. This point person serves as a central coordinator, liaising with vendors, assisting with logistics, and addressing any unforeseen issues that may arise.

Crafting a detailed timeline requires careful consideration and collaboration, but its implementation ensures that your wedding day unfolds seamlessly, allowing you to savor every precious moment without worrying about logistical challenges.

DELEGATING TASKS AND RESPONSIBILITIES

On the day of your wedding, managing logistics efficiently can make all the difference in ensuring a smooth and memorable experience. Delegating tasks and responsibilities is a strategic approach that empowers individuals to focus on their designated roles, contributing to the overall success of the event.

Establish a clear chain of command by appointing a reliable point person or wedding coordinator who can oversee the day's activities. This individual will serve as the central point of contact for vendors, guests, and the wedding party, alleviating stress and allowing the couple to fully immerse themselves in the celebration.

Divide tasks among trusted family members, friends, or members of the wedding party based on their strengths and expertise. Assign specific roles such as managing the gift table, coordinating transportation, or overseeing the ceremony and reception venues. Provide clear instructions and timelines to ensure everyone understands their responsibilities and knows who to turn to for guidance.

Communication is key throughout the day, so establish channels for staying in touch, whether through walkie-talkies, group messaging apps, or designated meeting points. Regular check-ins with key personnel can help address any issues promptly and keep the schedule on track.

Empower your team by expressing gratitude and acknowledging their contributions. A well-coordinated effort relies on the dedication and support of everyone involved, and recognizing their hard work fosters a sense of camaraderie and ensures a day filled with love and joy.

TIPS FOR STAYING CALM AND ENJOYING YOUR SPECIAL DAY

On your wedding day, managing day-of logistics is crucial for a smooth and enjoyable experience. *Here are some tips to help you stay calm and make the most of your special day:*

Create a Detailed Timeline: Develop a comprehensive schedule outlining key events, such as hair and makeup appointments, ceremony start time, and reception entrance. Share this timeline with your vendors, bridal party, and key family members to ensure everyone is on the same page.

Delegate Responsibilities: Assign specific tasks to trusted friends or family members to handle logistics on the day of the wedding. Whether it's overseeing setup at the venue, coordinating transportation, or managing vendor arrivals, delegating responsibilities can alleviate stress and allow you to focus on enjoying the moment.

Prepare an Emergency Kit: Pack a bridal emergency kit with essentials such as safety pins, stain remover, tissues, and pain relievers. Having these items on hand can help you tackle any unexpected mishaps with ease.

Designate a Point of Contact: Choose a reliable person, such as your wedding planner or maid of honor, to be the point of contact for vendors and guests on the day of the wedding. This individual can field questions, handle last-minute changes, and ensure that everything runs smoothly behind the scenes.

Practice Mindfulness Techniques: Incorporate mindfulness techniques, such as deep breathing or meditation, to stay grounded and calm throughout the day. Take moments to pause, reflect, and soak in the joyous atmosphere surrounding you.

CONCLUSION

"The Ultimate Wedding Planner: Your Guide to Creating the Perfect Day" serves as an indispensable resource for couples embarking on the journey of wedding planning. Throughout this guide, we have explored every aspect of crafting a memorable and personalized wedding experience. From setting budgets and selecting venues to designing décor and managing day-of logistics, each chapter offers practical advice and actionable tips to ensure a seamless and joyful celebration.

One of the most crucial elements discussed in this guide is the process of selecting a wedding theme. Your chosen theme serves as the foundation for your entire wedding aesthetic, reflecting your unique style and personality as a couple. By carefully considering your interests, cultural background, and desired atmosphere, you can choose a theme that resonates deeply and creates a cohesive experience for you and your guests.

Ultimately, "The Ultimate Wedding Planner" empowers couples to navigate the complexities of wedding planning with confidence and grace, enabling them to create a day that is truly perfect in every way.

www.ingramcontent.com/pod-product-compliance
Lightning Source LLC
Chambersburg PA
CBHW081958260726
48659CB00009BA/3032